Mysterious You

Burp!

The most interesting book you'll ever read about eating

Written by Diane Swanson

Illustrated by Rose Cowles

Kids Can Press

A huge vote of thanks goes to Delane Peters, pediatrics nutritionist at the Victoria General Hospital, for her careful and thoughtful review of this book, to Vancouver freelance food stylist Joanne Facchin for sharing some of the intriguing tricks of her trade, to the Dial-A-Dietitian Nutrition Information Society of British Columbia for patient and informed responses to my questions and to the many scientists whose painstaking research helped me understand some of the marvels of the eating process. As well, I am grateful to my co-conspirators in this book — Val Wyatt for her editorial guidance and ever-ready wit and Rose Cowles for her fun, perfectly off-the-wall illustrations.

Kids Can Press acknowledges the financial support of the Ontario Arts Council, the Canada Council for the Arts and the Government of Canada, through the CBF, for our publishing activity.

Published in Canada by
Kids Can Press Ltd.
25 Dockside Drive
Toronto, ON M5A 0B5

Published in the U.S. by
Kids Can Press Ltd.
2250 Military Road
Tonawanda, NY 14150

www.kidscanpress.com

Edited by Valerie Wyatt
Designed by Marie Bartholomew

Medical clip art on pages 22, 23 (bottom right), 26 and 31 from LifeART image © 1998 William & Wilkins. All rights reserved.

The hardcover edition of this book is smyth sewn casebound.
The paperback edition of this book is limp sewn with a drawn-on cover.
Manufactured in Buji, Shenzhen, China, in 8/2014 by WKT Company

CM 01 0 9 8 7 6 5 4 3 2 1
CM PA 01 15 14 13 12 11 10

Library and Archives Canada Cataloguing in Publication
Swanson, Diane, 1944 –
      Burp! : the most interesting book you'll ever read about eating

(Mysterious you)
Includes index.

ISBN 978-1-55074-599-3 (bound)
ISBN 978-1-55074-601-3 (pbk.)

1. Digestion – Juvenile literature. I. Cowles, Rose, 1967–   .
II. Series: Mysterious you (Toronto, Ont.).

QP145.S94 2001   j612.3   C00-931635-3

Kids Can Press is a [orus™ Entertainment company

Contents

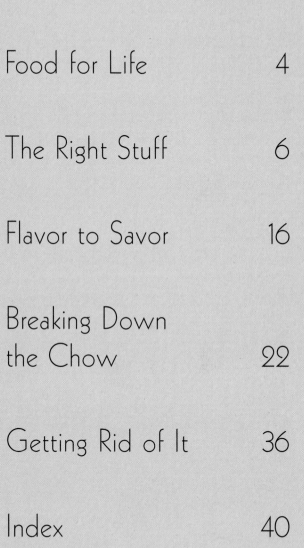

Food for Life

Michel Lotito of France ate for a living. Not a bad job, except for the menu: bicycles, TVs, computers, supermarket carts, chandeliers, a wooden coffin (empty) and an entire Cessna light airplane. He was not called Monsieur Mangetout (Mr. Eat Everything) for nothing.

Fairs and exhibitions paid Lotito to perform by eating odd stuff, but he would've eaten it anyway. He felt he must. It was a need that had driven him since he was nine, when he started nibbling glass and metal.

Lotito used patience and concentration while he ate "nonfood." He spent 15 days consuming a bicycle as a mound of metal filings and stewed tires, and 4 ½ days devouring a supermarket cart. Of course, it helped that his stomach lining was twice as thick as the average person's.

But Michel Lotito couldn't have eaten for a living if he didn't also eat to live. Like you, he needed regular food every day — meals that contain all the raw materials the body requires to operate and build, maintain and repair itself. Simply put, if Lotito didn't eat enough of the right kinds of food, he couldn't have lived. Neither could you.

- In 1980, a Chicago radio station ran a contest called "What's the Most Outrageous Thing You Would Do?" The winner, 19-year-old Jay Gwaltney, spent 89 hours eating a birch tree 3.4 m (11 ft.) tall.

- During its first two days of life, the larva of the polyphemus moth eats 86 000 times its birth weight in food.

You're No Dandelion

When it comes to giving your body what it needs, you're not as efficient as the average dandelion. Plants have it easy — they simply make their own meals. They take energy from the sun and use it to manufacture food out of water and carbon dioxide from the air. What's more, that food is already in a form the plant can use.

Now consider all the fuss and bother you go through. You must hunt, raise or buy food and prepare much of it before you can eat. Your body has to work for hours and hours to break food into a size and form that can enter the trillions of microscopic cells making up your body. Only then can you use food to build and repair yourself and to provide energy for all the things you do.

Eating Fast

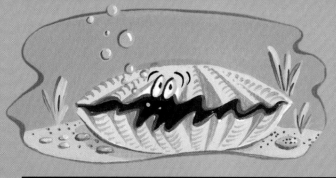

Some folks just can't resist setting records and winning bets — even if it means bolting down food as fast as they can. Speed-eater Thomas Carson of Illinois once proved he could devour 22 hamburgers and 2 L (2 qt.) of ice cream in only 25 minutes. Not to be outdone, Washington's Dave Barnes swallowed 424 clams in 8 minutes. England's Peter Dowdeswell ate 62 pancakes — with butter and syrup — in less than 7 minutes. And New York's Steve Meltzer gobbled up 96 sausages in 6 minutes. Amazing, but not recommended. Eating food that fast can make you choke, and it's tough on your digestive system.

The Right Stuff

Before Joe Murphy led his American team on a climb up China's tallest mountain in 1982, he planned the meals carefully. Having enough food, and the right kinds of food, was critical. The climb up Gongga Shan would take six weeks. To make it up the mountain and to keep warm in the freezing temperatures, the climbers would need plenty of fuel. Every day, each person would use about 5000 calories, or units of food energy — about twice what many adults normally need. For the seven-member team, that meant packing 570 kg (1250 lb.) of food, but it was worth it. Two members actually reached the summit, 7595 m (24 900 ft.) up, and everyone returned alive.

You can't climb mountains if your body is out of fuel. You can't do much else either. You burn about 35 calories just pounding a computer keyboard for 15 minutes. When you're sleeping, you use about 65 calories an hour. That's why it is so important to eat enough food every day.

It's also necessary to eat a wide variety of things. No one kind of food supplies all the nutrients and fiber (mostly cell walls of plants) that you need. Your body cells use six main types of nutrients — carbohydrates, proteins, fats, water, vitamins and minerals — in different ways so you can lead a healthy, active life.

The Energizers

Carbohydrates put the punch in your day. They provide more than half the energy you need to keep warm and to power your body and its systems. That's why you should devour a lot of carbs. Bread, rice, pasta and potatoes are rich in carbohydrates.

You'll also find plenty of carbs in sweets, such as cookies. But many foods that don't taste sweet still contain sugars. These carbohydrates provide energy almost instantly. There are different sugars, including sucrose from sugarcane and sugar beets, fructose from fruits and honey, and lactose from milk. The most plentiful kind is glucose from both plants and animals.

Most glucose comes from starch, a carbohydrate that plants such as wheat manufacture. When you consume wheat products, including bread and pasta, your body breaks down the starch into glucose. What you don't use right away is turned into another carb, called glycogen, and stored. Then, when you need more energy, your body breaks down the glycogen and gives you a boost of glucose.

- **Unlike a reptile's body temperature, yours is usually higher than the temperature of the air around you. Making that heat costs you calories, but it also keeps you warm.**

- **People in cold places usually eat more than people in hot places. They need extra food to keep their body temperature up.**

Brain Food

It takes energy to move your muscles. But did you know it also takes a lot of calories to power your brain? The brain's billions of cells are busy all the time. Run low on fuel, and they are the first to suffer. You feel tired and sluggish, and you have trouble concentrating.

First thing in the morning, your brain is truly starving. That's why it is so important to eat right away. Kids who jump-start their brains with breakfast do better at math and language exercises. Breakfast eaters also seem to have sharper memories and handle new information better.

The Builders

Proteins are power nutrients. They help the carbohydrates you eat produce the energy you need. But mostly, proteins are strong construction workers. Throughout your body, they labor day by day, building and repairing your many cells.

There are thousands of different proteins. Some form tough building material in muscles, nerves, skin and hair. Others, called enzymes, throw all sorts of chemical reactions into high gear — including the ones that help digest your dinner. Enzymes are so good at their jobs that they can speed up reactions thousands — even millions — of times. Still other kinds of proteins are hormones such as insulin, which works to control the sugar level in your blood.

Break up a single protein and you will find its basic building blocks, called amino acids. Your body needs about 20 different types of amino acids, and it can make most of them. The rest, called essential amino acids, come from what you eat. Animal food, such as meat, fish and cheese, contains all the essential amino acids, but most plants do not. That's why it is important to eat special veggie combos, such as rice and soya beans, if you're a vegetarian. The essential amino acids from different veggies combine to give you what you need.

- The tiny house-dust mite prefers low-fat food. Before eating dandruff, the mite often waits until a fungus has reduced the fat content.

- Japanese sumo wrestlers stuff themselves, then nap so they don't burn more calories than they have to. The average sumo champion weighs about 160 kg (350 lb.).

The Bankers

Like proteins and carbohydrates, fats provide an energy boost. In fact, a gram (0.035 oz.) of fat packs twice as much "oomph" as a gram of carbos. On days when you take in more calories than you use, the surplus may be deposited as fat and held until you need it. Then, if you run short of energy, your body can make a withdrawal from this "fat bank." Fat deposits do other jobs, too. They shield some of your bones and organs from injury. They also insulate your body to keep heat in.

There are two main fats in foods — saturated and unsaturated. Much of the saturated fat comes from animal foods, such as meats, eggs and cheeses. You get unsaturated fat from plants, such as corn and peanuts.

Although you need to eat fat every day — even to dissolve some of the vitamins you get — you shouldn't overdo it. You especially have to watch saturated fats. They could overload your bank reserves and clog your blood vessels with goop called cholesterol.

You Try It

Hiking burns up a lot of energy. Next time you go, pack a snack rich in carbohydrates, proteins and fats. Then your body can refuel fast. Here's a recipe for "Birdseed" from the Scouts. It's easy to mix and light to carry. Just toss together a handful of each of the following:

- raisins
- sugar-coated dry cereal (any kind you like)
- small chocolate candies or chocolate chips
- peanuts or cashew nuts

The Stream of Life

You take in water with every drink and every mouthful of food. Yes, there's water in all the plant and animal food you devour. That's lucky for you because water makes up the bulk of your body — as much as 75 percent of your weight.

Unlike carbohydrates, proteins and fats, water has no energy value. But of all the nutrients you need, it's the most important. For starters, your body depends on water to help break down the carbohydrates, proteins and fats you eat. It also helps move most other nutrients around the body in your bloodstream. It even dissolves wastes.

Just as rusty hinges seize up without oil, your joints wouldn't move smoothly without water. Nor would your body find it easy to keep a steady temperature. Water helps by holding heat in or cooling you off through sweat.

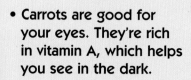

- Carrots are good for your eyes. They're rich in vitamin A, which helps you see in the dark.

- After World War I, British doctor Harriette Chick used vitamin D to cure many Austrian children of a bone disease called rickets and to prevent others from getting it.

The Supporters

Not everything you eat plays a leading role in nourishing your body. Still, you'd be in big trouble without the support of two nutrients — vitamins and minerals — and some fiber.

Many enzymes can't do their work without the help of small amounts of vitamins and minerals. For instance, the vitamin niacin, in meat, fish and cereals, helps make enzymes that maintain healthy body tissues. The mineral manganese, in vegetables, nuts and grains, triggers many different enzymes, including those that help you grow.

Besides these roles, there's a host of other duties that vitamins and minerals perform. Vitamin C, found in oranges, tomatoes and leafy vegetables, helps heal sores and wounds, while vitamin B1 (also called thiamine), in grains, peas and beans, works to release energy from carbohydrates. The mineral calcium, in dairy foods, green vegetables and nuts, builds strong bones and teeth, while iron, in meat, dried fruits and nuts, is important for healthy blood.

You can't digest all fiber found in foods such as bread, cereals, vegetables and fruits. But it's very important to your body. There are two main types — soluble and insoluble. Soluble fiber helps reduce blood cholesterol. Insoluble fiber makes your solid wastes bulky enough for you to get rid of them easily.

You Try It

Be a medical researcher. Track the number of servings of milk or milk products, such as yogurt, that every person in your family has each day. Record your findings for a week, figure out the daily average and compare it with what's recommended by nutrition experts below. Notice how age affects these recommendations.

Recommended Daily Minimum Servings of Milk or Milk Products

Age	Servings
Under 9	2
9 to 12	3 or 4
Teens	3 or 4
Adults	2 or 3

Note: A serving size is about 250 mL (1 c.).

Too Much

When it comes to food, you can have too much of a good thing. The amount you need each day depends mostly on your age, size, gender, general health and activities.

Eating more than you require can gradually make you overweight, or even obese — too fat to be healthy. Excess weight increases the risk of suffering serious illnesses, such as heart disease and diabetes. It can also strain muscles, bones and joints. Each kilogram (2 lb.) of extra weight in your body increases the pressure on your knee joints about six times.

Eating too much of one kind of food isn't good for you either. It's healthiest to have a balanced diet containing all the nutrients and fiber you need. Many nutrition experts recommend that, when you're 9 to 12, you have — each day — one or two servings of meat or meat substitutes such as beans, six servings of fruits and vegetables, six servings of bread and cereals, and three or four servings of milk or milk products.

You don't need a lot of vitamin pills if you eat a balanced diet. In fact, it's possible to overdose on vitamins. Most can be stored in your body, and a serious buildup makes you ill.

Too Little

If you don't eat enough food, you become tired, weak and unable to fight off diseases. Your body may start to devour itself. It may steal calcium from your bones when you run short, or take amino acids from your muscles if you're not eating the right amounts or kinds of proteins. Getting too few vitamins can also cause problems, including weak bones, mental illness and death. And if you're eating too little fat, you can't dissolve all the vitamins you need.

For some people, undereating is an illness called anorexia nervosa. They eat far too little to be healthy. Even though anorexics are too thin, they are terrified of being fat. Some literally starve themselves to death.

Never let fear of being — or becoming — overweight keep you from eating enough. Movies, magazines and store windows often present very slender bodies as "ideal," making many ordinary-sized people feel unhappy with their weight. But if clothing-store mannequins were to come alive, they wouldn't survive. They would have only half the body fat they'd need.

So be smart — eat the right amounts of the right stuff and use up excess calories through exercise.

- **The brains of babies who are well nourished are often larger than the brains of babies who are fed poorly for a long time.**

- **Rats will eat almost anything — even shoes — but they would rather eat a well-balanced meal of grains, vegetables, fruits, meats and cheeses.**

Eating Full-time

When his weight peaked at 543 kg (1197 lb.), Walter Hudson of New York was as big around as a bull. His waist — one of the world's largest — measured 302 cm (119 in.). Hudson used the bulk of his time to eat. For breakfast, he might have 12 eggs, 32 sausages, 454 g (1 lb.) of bacon and a loaf of bread. Lunch was often several hefty hamburgers plus a mountain of fries. In a single dinner, he might consume as many as 5 steaks, 6 whole potatoes, 4 heads of broccoli or 6 cobs of corn, and an entire pie. Between meals, he ate plenty of snacks.

Too big to move much, Hudson spent most of his 47 years in bed, where he died in 1991.

Powerful Cravings

Boiled briefcases, lipstick, sawdust and plaster made for bizarre food in 1941, when war trapped 3 million starving people in Leningrad, Russia. More recently, thousands of people desperately ill from a toxic environment in northern Uzbekistan (south of Russia) have been eating clay, chalk, threads from their clothing — even knitting needles.

Emergencies such as food shortages or illnesses can force people to eat strange things. But other people actually choose the unusual. The craving for nonfoods, called pica (PIE-kuh), has been recorded for centuries.

No one knows what causes pica. It appears more often among people who are poorly nourished, especially those who don't get enough of the mineral iron. They may crave chalk, hair, mothballs or toilet paper, but most commonly, they crave clay. Unfortunately, while rich in minerals, clay can actually make it harder for the body to absorb iron.

- People who crave ice often need iron, but ice adds mostly water to their diet.

- In Peru, colorful parrots called macaws eat clay from riverbanks, probably for the salt and other minerals. Eating clay may also help macaws get rid of poisons from some of the seeds they eat.

Regular Cravings

Have you ever experienced a food craving? Cravings for regular food are common, but hard to understand. There's no simple explanation for the urge to eat chocolate, for example. It doesn't seem to be a response to a bodily need, such as a shortage of magnesium. If it was, you might crave wheat germ (a richer source of magnesium) rather than chocolate. Some chemicals found in chocolate give you a feeling of pleasure, which may encourage you to eat it. Chocolate's smooth texture and the fact that it melts in your mouth also make it appealing. You may even crave chocolate because it reminds you of happy times. Or — who knows — maybe you just like the taste!

Sad Snack

It's rare to see shirt collars stiffened with laundry starch anymore. So what keeps this product on store shelves? Some people — mostly women with low incomes and poor nutrition — crave it as food.

Sadly, this craving makes a person's health even worse. Laundry starch is not packaged as food, so it can contain a lot of bacteria. It's also filling — especially for people who eat up to 1 kg (2 lb.) of it a day — so it reduces the appetite for food that's more nutritious. And laundry starch makes it hard for the body to absorb iron. Too little of this mineral causes weakness, dizziness and shortness of breath.

Flavor to Savor

Ever thought a city tastes like toast? That the color pink smells like angel food cake? Some people do. Others sniff textures, feel smells and hear colors. One man sees food flavors as shapes. To him, roasted chicken can be pointed (yummy) or round (not so yummy). He even senses the texture, weight and temperature of flavors. Sour flavors seem to slap his face or sting his fingertips.

The overlapping of senses in unusual ways is called synesthesia (sin-es-THEE-zha). It's so rare that only ten in a million people ever experience it. Although your senses probably don't overlap, you use all of them to get information about the food you eat. You see colors and forms, smell and taste flavors, feel temperatures and textures — even hear sounds when you bite into food.

Your ability to sense your meals affects how and what you eat. Your appetite is also influenced by thoughts and feelings and by the people, places and objects around you.

- Many restaurant chefs in Japan arrange different foods in the same meal in unmatched dishes. The shape, color and design of each plate or bowl flatters the food it holds.

- Food photographers can use 20 pizzas in setting up one perfect shot for an advertisement.

Say Cheeseburger!

To Your Eye, In Your Ear

That hamburger you see in TV commercials may be just for show. With the help of a plumber's blowtorch, the meat can be browned on the outside and made to sizzle. It's also injected with oil and water for a wonderfully juicy look. The cheese is likely melted — ever so gently — with a wallpaper steamer. And a hose releases vapor, so the burger appears to be piping hot.

Companies spend top dollars to make food look great on TV. And chefs take pains to present attractive meals in restaurants. They know how important it is to make your mouth water and your stomach juices flow, so that you want to eat.

Russian scientist Ivan Pavlov (1849–1936) proved that just a single sense, such as sight, could stimulate the appetite. In one of his experiments, dogs drooled when they saw food. So strong is this effect that even imagining a juicy burger or a fudge sundae can make your mouth water.

Put the power of eye and ear appeal to the test:

- The next time your family is having mashed potatoes, color some with flavorless green or blue food dye. Does the difference in color make anyone sense a difference in flavor? Notice if anyone eats a smaller portion than usual. Ask why.

- Close your eyes and think hard about your favorite food. Imagine how it looks — its color, shape, thickness and size. Remember how it sounds as you take a bite. Does your mouth water when you concentrate on this picture? Ask a friend to do the same thing, then compare notes.

Over Your Tongue, Up Your Nose

Thousands of taste buds on your tongue, the roof of your mouth and the back of your throat help you taste food. In each of these buds, there are tiny cells tipped with hairs. The cells respond to tastes when food is moistened and molecules are dissolved by the watery saliva in your mouth. Then they send messages about what they've discovered along nerves to your brain.

Different taste buds are more sensitive to certain tastes than to others. Some are best at detecting sweet flavors, others at salty. Some home in on sour tastes, others on bitter.

Your sense of smell detects flavors even more than your sense of taste. Odor molecules enter your nose directly from the food on your plate. As you chew the food, you release more odor molecules, which travel from the back of your mouth into your nose. The molecules dissolve in a lining of watery mucus and stimulate tiny hairs embedded there. Then the hairs send odor messages to the brain.

Meanwhile, dense crowds of sensors on the surface of your tongue are also working hard. While you're eating, they are busy feeling the texture of the food and detecting its temperature. Your brain takes messages it receives from these sensors and adds them to what arrived from your nose and taste buds. It combines them all to create the flavors you experience.

Expiry Date: July 4, 2012

Sense the Difference

Food doesn't look, taste, smell, feel and sound the same to everybody. In fact, what you think is great to eat may seem awful to a friend. The senses you inherit from your parents explain some of this difference; so does your experience with different foods. Just the sight of whipped cream could turn your stomach if you threw up the last time you ate it.

Even age causes differences in senses. For instance, you probably have a keener sense of taste than your parents. Most children have extra taste buds in their cheeks, but lose them when they become teenagers.

Besides the pleasures of food, your senses can alert you to the dangers. If you popped some poisonous berries in your mouth, their bitter taste would likely make you gag and spit them out. Taste buds that detect bitterness are about 10 000 times more sensitive than buds that detect sweetness — for good reason.

Your smell sensors work even better. They can pick up the scent of rotting meat well before you put it in your mouth. Imagine the grief that can save you.

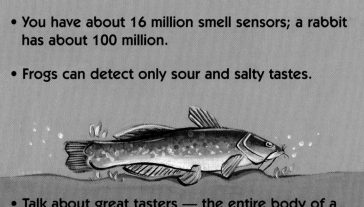

- **You have about 16 million smell sensors; a rabbit has about 100 million.**

- **Frogs can detect only sour and salty tastes.**

- **Talk about great tasters — the entire body of a brown bullhead, a North American freshwater fish, is covered with taste buds.**

You Try It

- **Hit your smell sensors right on:**
  Lean over a bowl of hot soup, breathe normally and notice the smell. Sit back, then lean over again and breathe very deeply. Is the smell stronger? That's because you are drawing the odor right to your sensors.

- **Taste a smell:**
  Open a bottle of strong cologne and smell it. Notice how the odor moves through your nose into your mouth and stimulates your taste buds. Yuck!

- **Discover how smell and sight affect taste:**
  Ask someone to place peeled cubes of raw potato, turnip and apple on a plate. Close your eyes, hold your nose and taste each cube. Can you tell which is which?

All in Your Mind ...

Besides the messages from your senses, your feelings and thoughts can also affect your interest in eating. Long-lasting sadness, an illness called depression, can cause people to produce less saliva and eat less. But if they have been dieting, their depression has the opposite effect — it can make them eat more.

People, places and objects in your life also affect what, how much and when you eat. For instance, you tend to eat more around people who are eating, even if you're not hungry. And you tend to eat less around those who are eating little or nothing — even if you're very hungry.

Rooms that are clean and pleasant can awaken your appetite and make it easier to digest food. Even the colors of walls, tablecloths and decorations can affect your eating. Red may encourage you to eat more; blue, less. Pink may tempt you to eat sweet foods. And then there's the clock on the wall. If you usually eat at noon, just seeing the hands meet at 12 can make you want lunch — no matter how many snacks you've eaten that morning.

... Or Is It?

Never mind where you are, who you're with or what's going on in your life, sometimes you're just plain hungry. Your body has absorbed the last of the nutrients you gave it, you're running out of energy, and YOU WANT FOOD.

The hormone insulin checks the supply of available glucose in your system. When that supply runs low, the insulin sends a message to your brain, triggering your appetite.

Although glucose supplies are important in controlling your hunger in the short term — from meal to meal — fat plays a more important role in the long term. If you extend the usual time between meals, your body starts drawing on its fat bank for energy. That sends another signal to your brain to tell you that you're hungry.

- In experiments, the smell of banana or peppermint made some people less interested in eating.

- Canadians became keener to try pollack, a saltwater fish, after it was given a more pleasing name — Boston bluefish.

Can you make your family hungry?

- Play fast, loud music at some meals and slow, soft music at others. Does the music affect how fast your family eats? Some restaurants have discovered that fast, loud music excites people to eat quickly.

- One morning, secretly switch the time on a house clock from 11 to 12, then point out that it's noon. See if your family feels ready to eat lunch. (After your experiment, don't forget to change the clock back.)

- Just before dinner each day, play the same song. After two or three weeks, play the song a bit earlier and see if it triggers hunger in anyone in your family.

Breaking Down the Chow

A shooting accident in 1822 left 19-year-old Alexis St. Martin with a hole 5 cm (2 in.) wide leading right into his stomach. The French-Canadian fur trader recovered and lived to old age, but the hole never closed. For him, it was a nuisance, but for the rest of the world, it was a window into the human stomach. William Beaumont, the American doctor who first tended to St. Martin, studied him for years, solving some of the mysteries of how the stomach breaks down food.

As amazing as the workings of the stomach are, it takes much more to digest food. Nothing — not even a drop of orange juice — is small enough to enter one of your microscopic body cells. Every molecule in every speck of food must be subdivided, and its form must be converted, before your body can use it. For that, you need a whole system of digestive organs.

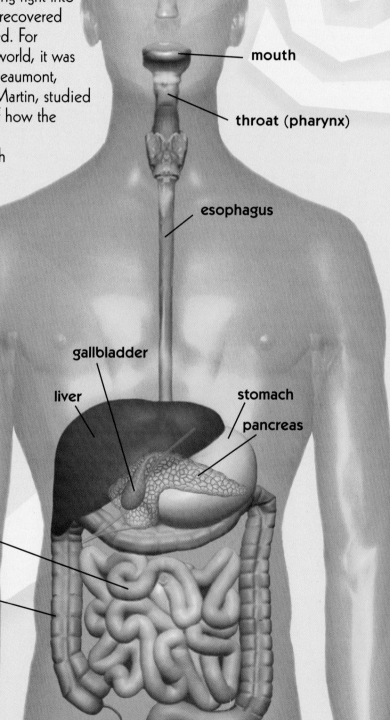

mouth

throat (pharynx)

esophagus

gallbladder

liver

stomach

pancreas

small intestine

large intestine

Winning Team

Meet the players in your remarkable digestive system. Your throat, esophagus, stomach, small intestine and large intestine together form a tube, or tract, up to 9 m (30 ft.) long. Other players work with this tract to help you digest food — your teeth, tongue, salivary glands, liver, gallbladder and pancreas. The team has impressive skills. As mechanical masters, they crack, crunch, squeeze and grind up food. As chemists, they use many different enzymes, water and acids to reduce and transform all the food you consume.

Still, it can take about 24 hours — even up to 48 — for your digestive system to break down a meal. And it's work that wouldn't be possible if the team didn't involve other body systems. For instance, your muscular system helps move food through the digestive tract. Your nervous system carries messages to and from your brain to regulate digestion. And your circulatory system delivers the nutrients your digestive system produces.

- **A python may eat 1 1/2 times its weight in food at one meal, then spend a few days digesting it.**

- **When caterpillars attack tomato plants, the plants fight back. They release proteins that upset the caterpillars' digestion.**

- **The human body produces about 7 L (7 qt.) of digestive juices each day.**

The Stomach Scouts

William Beaumont wasn't the only early scientist to explore the stomach. French naturalist René A. F. de Réaumur proved that the stomach does more than grind up food. In 1752, he put bird feed into small metal cylinders with holes in them. He attached cords to the cylinders and fed them to hawks. When Réaumur pulled the cylinders out, he saw that the food had been partly digested by chemicals produced inside the birds' stomachs.

In 1776, Italian scientist Lazzaro Spallanzani studied his own digestion. He put a piece of sponge in a small wire cage tied to a string and swallowed the cage. Then he pulled it up, squeezed out the stomach chemicals absorbed by the sponge, and used the chemicals to digest meat.

Chomping and Grinding

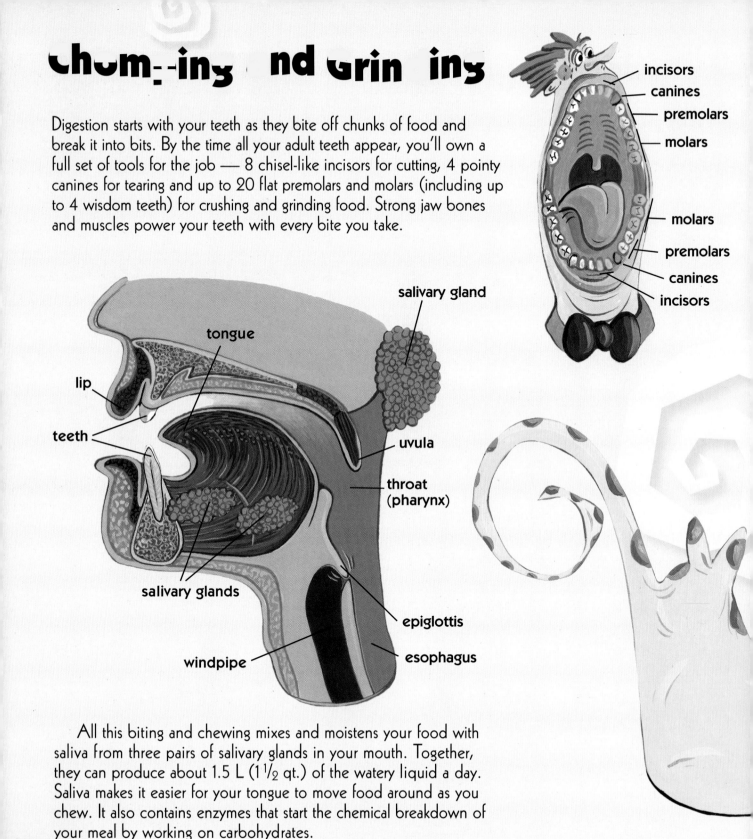

Digestion starts with your teeth as they bite off chunks of food and break it into bits. By the time all your adult teeth appear, you'll own a full set of tools for the job — 8 chisel-like incisors for cutting, 4 pointy canines for tearing and up to 20 flat premolars and molars (including up to 4 wisdom teeth) for crushing and grinding food. Strong jaw bones and muscles power your teeth with every bite you take.

incisors
canines
premolars
molars

molars
premolars
canines
incisors

salivary gland

tongue

lip

teeth

uvula

throat
(pharynx)

salivary glands

epiglottis

esophagus

windpipe

All this biting and chewing mixes and moistens your food with saliva from three pairs of salivary glands in your mouth. Together, they can produce about 1.5 L (1 1/2 qt.) of the watery liquid a day. Saliva makes it easier for your tongue to move food around as you chew. It also contains enzymes that start the chemical breakdown of your meal by working on carbohydrates.

Gulping and Passing

As you swallow, your muscular tongue pushes moist food to the back of your mouth. There, a flap of flesh — the uvula (YOO-vya-la) — rises to close off passages to the nose. That's a very good thing; otherwise, wet noodles might head the wrong way and slide up and out of your nostrils.

When a lump of food, called a bolus, starts down your throat, or pharynx, another important flap flips into action. Called the epiglottis, this flap covers your windpipe so that the bolus doesn't enter and make you choke. Food simply slips on by to the esophagus, a tube leading to the stomach. But the bolus doesn't just drop down the esophagus. Muscles contract and relax in a process called peristalsis (pair-e-STALL-ses), squeezing it along.

- A snake can unhinge its jaws and expand its esophagus to swallow prey much fatter than itself.

- The giant African snail, which can weigh 0.5 kg (1 lb.), has 80 000 teeth. It can eat a whole head of lettuce in less than 12 hours.

- At birth, all of your "baby" and adult teeth — not yet fully formed — were hidden in your gums.

You Try It

Investigate your own uvula. Grab a hand mirror and head for a bright light. Open wide and say "Ahhh." As you do, look for the little red flap hanging from the roof of your mouth, right at the back. That is your uvula.

Now see how fast your uvula can move when it has to. Watch what it does as you cough after saying "Ahhh." Think how hard swallowing would be if that handy flap wasn't there.

Storing and Churning

Your stomach is a J-shaped elastic sac that can stretch to hold about 1.5 L (1 1/2 qt.) of food. Its job as a storage tank is an important one. The stomach holds the food until the rest of your digestive system is ready for it. That means you can process meals slowly, nourishing your body cells throughout the day — not just after you eat.

That's not all. Millions of tiny stomach glands produce an enzyme called pepsin, which splits apart proteins in the food. The stomach glands also make digestive juices — mainly hydrochloric acid — that mix with the pepsin to help it work. Strong enough to dissolve razor blades, hydrochloric acid kills many of the bacteria living in your food. Fortunately, your stomach is protected by a mucus lining, which it replaces approximately every three days. Otherwise, your stomach might digest itself.

Strong muscles in the stomach's walls knead and churn your food to break it down even more. They mix it all up into a thick stew, then push it into the small intestine — a bit at a time. Rings of muscles, called sphincters, control the exit from the stomach — as they control the entrance to the stomach from the esophagus. After about four hours, your stomach is just hanging around again — empty.

esophagus

liver

stomach

pancreas

gallbladder

small intestine

large intestine

Juicing It Up

Three other organs in your body help the digestive tract work. Tucked behind your stomach, the little pancreas makes about 1.5 L (1 ½ qt.) of pancreatic juice each day. This juice flows into the small intestine, protecting it from any acid in the food coming from the stomach. The pancreas also produces and delivers enzymes that help break down proteins, carbohydrates and fats in the small intestine.

But these enzymes couldn't attack fats if it wasn't for your liver and gallbladder. Every day, the spongy liver — the biggest organ inside your body — produces about 1 L (1 qt.) of greenish yellow bile. It's a juice that turns fats into droplets so enzymes can go to work on them. The liver stores the bile in a little sac called the gallbladder, which releases it as needed. Luckily for you, your liver is very durable. It can function even if a big chunk is removed. What's more, it can rebuild itself within a few months.

- **Your stomach keeps itself in good shape. A scratch that takes a week to heal on your arm can heal in a day on your stomach.**

- **A cow's four-part stomach breaks down many plants more thoroughly than your one-part stomach does.**

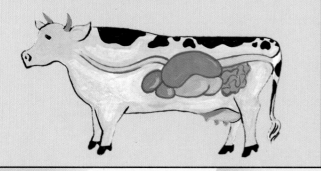

Gut Reactions

In ancient India, a crime suspect was given a handful of uncooked rice to chew, then spit out. If the rice was still dry, the suspect was found guilty. That's because the fear of being discovered was believed to be enough to make the mouth dry. Only one problem — the fear of being thought guilty could do the same thing.

Emotions can slow — or sometimes speed — the flow of saliva in the mouth. They also affect the stomach. Fear or unhappiness may even stop the stomach from working, and aggression may force it to release acids. People can become so upset that their stomach produces extra acid, which backs up into the esophagus. That produces a burning pain called heartburn, because you feel it close to your heart.

Completing and Absorbing

The small intestine is small in name only. It measures less than 4 cm (1 1/2 in.) across, but it's up to 7 m (23 ft.) long — coiled and folded to fit inside you. And its lining is an amazing 600 times longer than the intestine itself! That's because there are millions of tiny flaps, called villi, in the lining, and each one is covered by many smaller flaps. You would have to iron the lining and all its flaps out flat to see its total length.

Not only is the small intestine big in size, it does a truly big job. It creates the most powerful reactions in the entire digestive system. Using enzymes that it produces, as well as juices from the pancreas, liver and gallbladder, the small intestine does most of the work of pulling nutrients apart. It also attacks fats and completes the digestion of proteins and carbohydrates.

As peristalsis pushes and squeezes the mushy food mixture, the small intestine breaks it down even more. Slippery mucus on the walls of the small intestine helps the mush slide along, while protecting the intestine. Muscles press the mixture against the villi, which absorb the nutrients.

Sucking and Shaping

Ending the digestive tract is your large intestine, a tube about 6.5 cm (2 1/2 in.) across and 1.5 m (5 ft.) long. It gets the leftovers after your small intestine has removed many of the nutrients. The large intestine absorbs about 90 percent of the water in these undigested leftovers. It also absorbs salts and other nutrients, such as vitamin K, which is made by bacteria that live in wastes and in the intestine itself. Vitamin K helps your blood clot when you cut yourself, so you don't bleed to death.

Like the small intestine, the large intestine is lined with slimy mucus that protects its walls and helps the leftovers squeeze through. As they are reduced to waste, they're shaped into stools, ready for passing.

And the appendix? No one knows for sure what this dead-end tube, stuck to the first part of the large intestine, does. It might be the remains of an organ that was once quite big and likely helped our early ancestors digest grass.

- A tapeworm has no digestive system of its own. Instead, it hooks onto the intestine of an animal, such as you, and soaks up digested food there.

- Food can whiz through a bat in about 20 minutes. It takes more than 20 hours to pass through you.

Super Gear

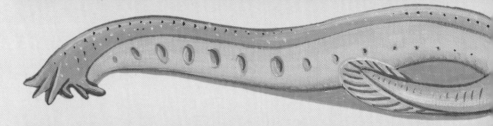

You may think your intestines are impressive, but consider the organs in these ocean critters.

The intestines of a primitive fish called the hagfish run from its throat to its back end. It gets no help from the stomach in digesting meals because it doesn't own one. The hagfish does, however, use a tooth-covered tongue to scrape its food to bits before swallowing.

Seals and sea lions in cold northern waters often have to keep their bodies about 38° C (100° F) warmer than ocean temperatures. To produce enough energy for heat, their digestive systems must be fast and efficient. Food can whiz through their bodies in only six hours, even though their intestines — proportional to their body length — are among the world's longest. The intestines of a hefty Steller's sea lion, for instance, can be 38 times longer than its body!

In the Cell—Finally!

You chomp, gulp and churn your food. You juice it up and break it down. You put your whole digestive system in motion to do one vital thing — nourish all the cells that make you what you are. These individual cells combine to form tissues, such as muscle tissues, which combine to form organs, such as your heart.

It's up to your blood to deliver nutrients to each of the cells in these tissues and organs. Blood picks up the nutrients that your intestines absorb and transports them throughout your body. As the blood flows past the cells in tiny vessels called capillaries, nutrients leak out through the capillaries' thin walls. The nutrients pass into the cells, where they are broken down, releasing energy and making new materials for growth and repair.

Your bloodstream does not feed every cell equally. Some cells need special nutrients or different mixes or amounts than others. And the cells in some tissues and organs need more regular feeding. Vital organs, such as your brain and heart, get first priority. You wouldn't want them shutting down for lack of food.

As cells break down nutrients, they create wastes, such as the gas carbon dioxide. These wastes leak out of the cells and into the capillaries. Then the blood carries carbon dioxide to your lungs to be exhaled and many other wastes to your kidneys to be expelled.

Hooray for the Special Chemists

If you didn't have a team of special chemists to fix up your blood before it makes deliveries to your cells, you'd be dead. The liver and pancreas, which also help you digest food, work hard to balance the many chemicals in your bloodstream.

Blood flowing through your intestines picks up harmful and useless molecules as well as many nutrients. The liver removes poisonous chemicals, such as caffeine in chocolate, and breaks them down. The blood can then dissolve them and carry them off to your kidneys to be expelled. The liver also stores iron, copper and several different vitamins, quickly sending them back to the bloodstream whenever they're needed. Among its many other jobs, the liver helps regulate your blood sugar level, absorbing extra glucose to store as glycogen, then releasing it when your blood sugar level is low.

The other special chemist, the pancreas, produces the insulin that helps keep blood sugar at a normal level. Insulin also makes sure that body cells get the amount of glucose they need.

> • Your body holds more blood than a big milk jug could — more than 5 L (5 qt.).

Always on the Go

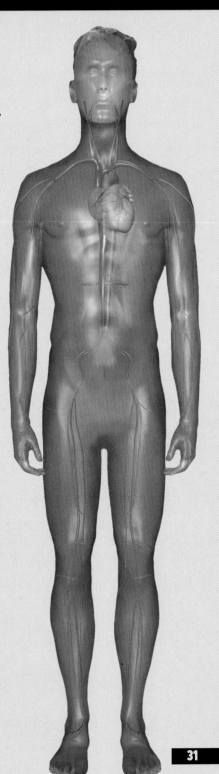

So powerful is your heart that your bloodstream reaches every cell you own in about a minute! That's a very good thing — nutrients are delivered quickly and regularly to all parts of your body.

Day in and day out, your heart operates two powerful pumps that send blood speeding on its way. The blood flows out through muscular vessels called arteries, which help push it along. It enters a vast network of capillaries that account for most of the bloodstream's route. Blood from these capillaries flows into veins, the vessels that guide it back to the heart. Unlike arteries, veins can't squeeze. But big muscles in your legs push against veins to help return blood to your heart.

To serve its trillions of body cell customers, blood must stream through approximately 100 000 km (62 000 mi.) of vessels. That's a journey more than 2 ½ times longer than a trip around Earth.

The major arteries (in red) and veins (in blue) of the body are shown here. There are many more smaller ones.

Down It Flows

About 200 times a day, all of your blood runs through your kidneys — two small, bean-shaped organs built for heavy-duty cleaning. The kidneys filter out extra salts and water and the waste your cells produce. Much of this waste can be poisonous.

The kidneys reabsorb most of the liquid and any other useful matter. This "good stuff" is passed back to the blood for use in the body. The kidneys release the "bad stuff" — a mixture of wastes — as urine, about 1.5 L (1 ½ qt.) of it each day.

Drop by drop, the urine travels through tubes into a stretchy storage bag called the bladder. Sensors in your bladder walls let you know when it's almost full, which gives you time to head for the bathroom.

Why is urine yellow? Some of the cells in the digestive system absorb yellow coloring from bile and pass it on.

- Even if your bladder is nearly empty, stress can cause its muscles to tighten, making you want to "go."

- Face flies hang around cows, feeding on various liquids they produce, including urine.

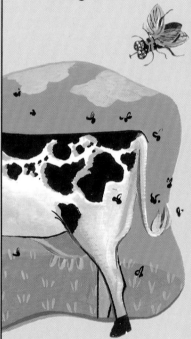

- Rabbits get more nutrients from their food by eating it twice, so they nibble their own stools.

Out It Goes

Solid waste from your digestive system ends up in the rectum, the short bottom section of your large intestine. The rectum holds your stools until you get rid of them. The solid stuff is a mucky mix of dead body cells, bacteria — both dead and alive — and food you can't digest, such as fibers from plants. And water — in fact, stools are mostly water.

Like urine, stools are colored by bile. They're brown, not yellow, because they absorb a different coloring material from the bile. Solid waste can be toxic, so it's good to get rid of it.

When your body senses viruses or other problems in its digestive system, it tries to drive them out — fast. It rushes food through the intestines without giving cells time to absorb enough water. That leaves you with runny stools, or diarrhea. Stress can have the same effect. It can make muscles in your intestines squeeze in ways that make some people say they feel "all tied up in knots."

When waste isn't bulky enough to prod the intestines into action, it moves along too slowly. Then cells have time to absorb even more water than normal. You end up with dry, hard stools that you can't pass easily — you're constipated.

You Try It

Be prepared. Mix up the drinks below if diarrhea strikes. It's important to replace the water — and some of the salts and sugars — that the body loses through diarrhea. These quick and easy drinks will help.

- **Sweet Sea Suzy**
  Stir and dissolve 5 mL (1 tsp.) of sugar and a pinch of salt in 1 L (1 qt.) of water. Mmm, not bad.

- **Honey Apple Blossom**
  Stir and dissolve 2.5 mL ($\frac{1}{2}$ tsp.) of honey and a pinch of salt in 250 mL (1 c.) of apple juice. Mmm, even better.

Case of Mistaken Identity

Card playing usually isn't considered dangerous, but one man was attacked by food while having a game with his son. Hours earlier, the man's son had snacked on some shrimp, which his father was highly allergic to. As they were playing cards, traces of the shrimp passed from the son's hands to the cards, then to the father's hands. When the man casually rubbed his eyes, the shrimp entered his body. That's all it took to set off an allergic reaction.

A food allergy is really a case of mistaken identity. The body wrongly labels one or more of the proteins in a particular food as an enemy invader. The immune system — special cells that fight germs, viruses and bacteria — jumps into action, sending proteins called antibodies to search for the invader. Then it releases chemicals to destroy the enemy.

The problem is that these chemicals irritate parts of the body, such as the digestive system. Swelling, vomiting and diarrhea are common reactions. They can be mild or severe, but fortunately, they aren't usually very strong the first time people eat food they're allergic to.

The Offenders

Almost any kind of food can produce an allergic reaction, but most of the trouble comes from the proteins in cow's milk, wheat, egg whites, soya beans, nuts (especially peanuts), fish and shellfish (shrimp, crab, lobster). People with food allergies are often allergic to two or three different foods and to some nonfoods, such as pollen and dust.

Food allergies can be so strong that contact with just 0.001 mL (1/5000 tsp.) of the offending food can cause death within 15 minutes. Up to eight percent of children have food allergies, but many outgrow them. Only about two percent of adults have true food allergies.

There is no cure for food allergies, so people who suffer from them must be very careful to avoid foods that trigger attacks.

- **People can be allergic to apples, but usually only to the skin.**

People with food allergies must read product labels carefully. Their lives may depend on it. The labels are supposed to list everything that the products contain.

Check the contents of your fridge and kitchen cupboards. See how many labels list ingredients that commonly cause problems for people with food allergies— milk, wheat flour, egg whites, soya beans or nuts. These ingredients can pop up in some unexpected places. Can you spot any labels that include special warnings for people with food allergies?

Getting Rid of It

"Men eat to vomit and vomit to eat," said a Roman leader about 2000 years ago. Wealthy Romans of his time — both women and men — often ate until they nearly burst. They enjoyed huge feasts of fancy foods — jellyfish, ostrich, fish livers, flamingo tongues and pheasant brains. When they were too full to eat more, they ordered slaves to tickle inside their throats. That made the diners gag and vomit, emptying their stomachs so they could eat again.

Of course, most people don't "eat to vomit and vomit to eat," but their bodies do eliminate unwanted food and waste, including poisons. Regularly, that means getting rid of urine and stools. Rarely, it means vomiting.

Up It Comes

Overeating, dizziness — even fright — can cause you to vomit. More often, though, you throw up because your body is trying to get rid of a virus or toxin that may make you sick.

Vomiting often starts as far down as the upper part of your small intestine. Muscles around your middle squeeze, pushing partly digested food up and through the opening to your stomach. Then the muscles squeeze some more, squishing the stomach and forcing the slimy food up your esophagus to your mouth and out. Yuck!

Depending on how long the food has been digesting, the vomit is chunky or smooth, but it all tastes terrible. It's sour because some stomach acid backs up with the food. And it burns. Unlike your stomach, your esophagus has no lining to protect it from the strong acid.

- **Rats can't vomit. They don't have the necessary muscles.**

- **For centuries, rich people in Europe used "personal tasters" to check food for poison. That was a better way of getting rid of bad food than vomiting or diarrhea — but not for the taster, of course.**

- **Vultures feed on decaying flesh. Their vomit is so stinky that they sometimes use it to turn away their enemies.**

Oops — Gas!

Everybody carries around about 0.25 L (1 c.) of gas in the digestive system. The trouble is that the body usually picks up about 2.5 L (10 c.) of gas a day. Saliva carries tiny air bubbles to the stomach with each swallow. And the stomach and small intestine make gas when they can't digest certain carbohydrates in food such as beans, broccoli and fruit. When these carbohydrates move to the large intestine, bacteria break them down, producing gas. So what happens to the extra 2.25 L (9 c.) of gas? It pops out in small explosions as burps — or worse.

Food, Friends and Family

For centuries, several aboriginal tribes from eastern Australia gathered in the mountains to eat masses of moths that migrated there each summer. They cooked the insects in hot sand, or ground them into a paste to make cakes. The feasting lasted for weeks. It not only provided good nutrition, it gave the tribes an opportunity to exchange news, trade goods and enjoy one another's company.

Do you like eating with friends or family? Talking about your day at dinner? People have always liked to chow down together.

Even early humans sat around a fire to share the animal they hunted. They probably shared their stories too, which helped give them a sense of belonging.

Today, people in every country "break bread" with friends, setting out refreshments for company and inviting one another for dinner. They use food to help celebrate holidays, weddings and birthdays. It's hard to imagine a party without anything to eat.

Like everyone, you eat to live and stay healthy, but you also eat for the pleasure of being with friends and family.

Food for the Future

So what lies ahead? Will you eat much differently in coming decades than you do today? In some science-fiction stories, people pop pills instead of food. One meal-in-a-capsule provides all the nutrition they need in a day. If that came true, "eating" wouldn't be much of a social occasion.

But if the meals in spacecrafts are any indication, regular food will be popular for a long time. Astronauts once squeezed their food out of tubes. Later they ate meals that had been squished into cubes. The food was nutritional, but it wasn't satisfying. As technology made it possible to install fridges and ovens in spacecraft, astronauts returned to meals that resembled what they had at home.

Even if people of the future develop foods different from what we have today, they will likely prefer meals that offer more than nutrition. Company and food just seem to go together.

- In 1989, nine climbers from Australia held a top-of-the-world dinner party at the peak of Mt. Huascaran, Peru — over 6770 m (22 200 ft.) high. They climbed up with a table, chairs and a three-course meal!

- When peregrine falcons go courting, the male gives the female a gift of food — usually a dead bird.

- Chocolate Girl Guide cookies were a favorite snack for Roberta Bondar on her 1992 space journey as Canada's first female astronaut.

You Try It

Invite some friends to a "Wacky Dinner." Without saying what you're serving, hand them each a list of the colors of the items on your menu. (Some suggestions are below.) Have each guest number the colors in the order she or he wants to receive them. Then serve the dinner items — one at a time. Did anyone start with dessert? Who had to eat jelly, rice or beans before getting a spoon?

Colors	Dinner Items
White	Rice
Brown	Canned baked beans
Orange	Carrot sticks
Golden	Apple juice
Red	Strawberry jelly
Gray*	Spoon

*Saying "silver" would make it too easy.

Index